Published by Creative Education
and Creative Paperbacks
P.O. Box 227, Mankato, Minnesota 56002
Creative Education and Creative Paperbacks
are imprints of The Creative Company
www.thecreativecompany.us

Design by The Design Lab
Production by Travis Green
Art direction by Rita Marshall
Printed in the United States of America

Photographs by Corbis (Gallo Images), Dreamstime
(Alslutsky, Dennis Donohue, Isselee, Photowitch), Getty
Images (Michael Dunning; Gary Mezaros/Visuals Un-
limited, Inc.), iStockphoto (bibi57/Norbert Bieberstein,
spxChrome), National Geographic Creative (GEORGE
GRALL, THOMAS MARENT/MINDEN PICTURES),
SuperStock (Flirt, imageBROKER, Minden Pictures)

Library of Congress Cataloging-in-Publication Data
Bodden, Valerie.
Frogs / Valerie Bodden.
p. cm. — (Amazing animals)
Summary: A basic exploration of the appearance,
behavior, and habitat of frogs, the long-legged
amphibians that hop. Also included is a story from
folklore explaining why some frogs croak.
Includes bibliographical references and index.
ISBN 978-1-60818-611-2 (hardcover)
ISBN 978-1-62832-217-0 (pbk)
ISBN 978-1-56660-658-5 (eBook)
1. Frogs—Juvenile literature. I. Title. II. Series:
Amazing animals.
QL668.E2B5185 2016
597.8'9—dc23   2014048705

CCSS: RI.1.1, 2, 4, 5, 6, 7; RI.2.2, 5, 6, 7, 10;
RI.3.1, 5, 7, 8; RF.1.1, 3, 4; RF.2.3, 4

HC 9 8 7 6 5 4 3 2
First Edition PBK 9 8 7 6 5 4 3 2 1

AMAZING ANIMALS

FROGS

BY VALERIE BODDEN

CREATIVE EDUCATION • CREATIVE PAPERBACKS

Frogs are amphibians (*am-FIB-ee-uns*). Amphibians are **cold-blooded** animals that spend part of their lives in water and part on land. There are more than 5,000 kinds of frogs.

cold-blooded having bodies that are always as warm or as cold as the air around them

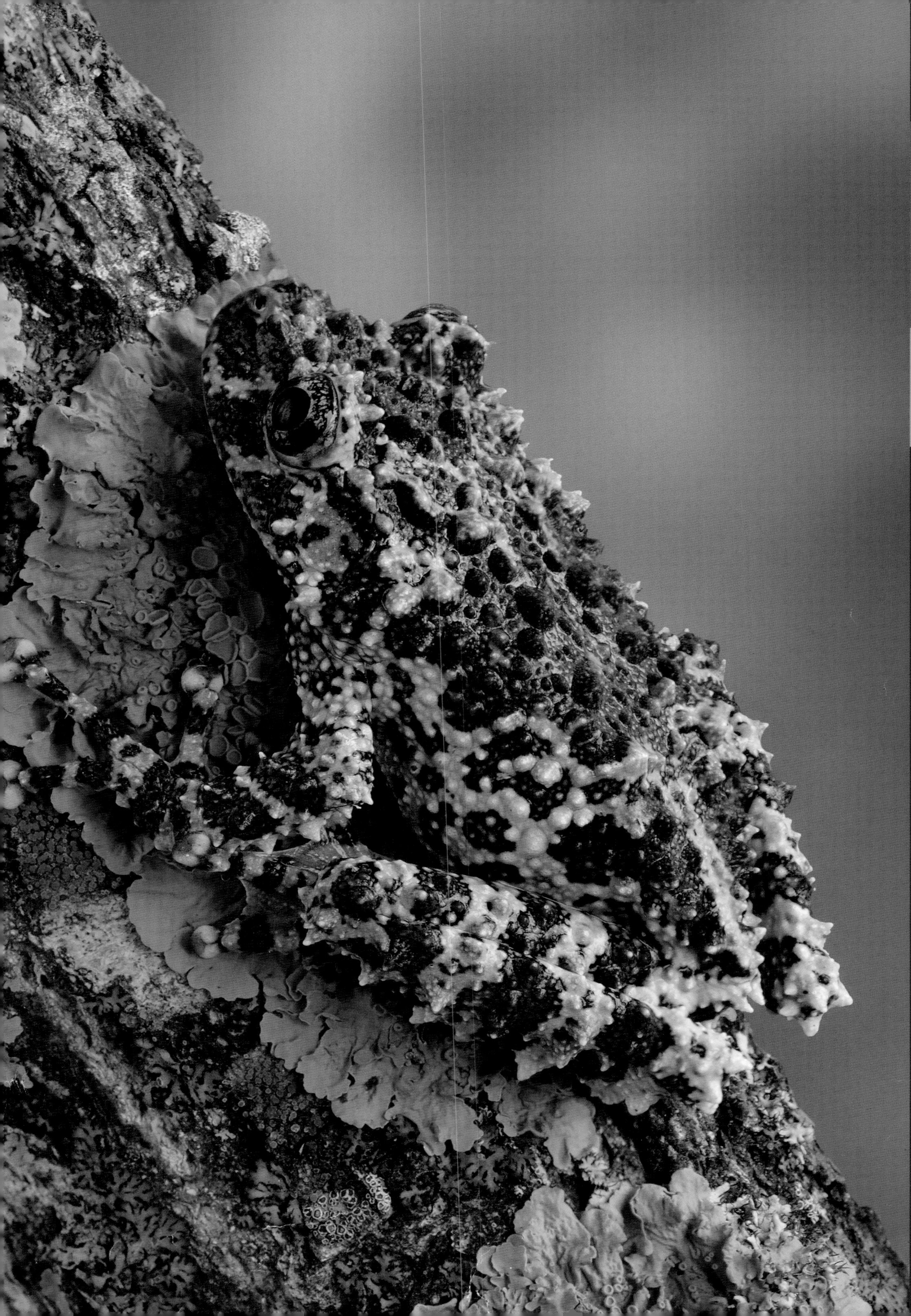

A red-eyed tree frog's toepads act like big suction cups

All frogs have wide, flat heads with bulging eyes. Their long back legs help them hop. Frogs that swim have **webbed** feet. But some tree frogs have sticky toepads to help them climb. Many frogs are gray, brown, or green. Others are bright colors.

webbed joined together by pieces of skin

The smallest frogs are tinier than your fingernail. But the biggest frogs can grow up to 35 inches (88.9 cm) long. They can weigh as much as a newborn baby!

Giant leaf frogs will grow up to five inches (12.7 cm) long

Some kinds of bullfrogs
hide underground
when it is cold or dry

Frogs live everywhere in the world except Antarctica. Some frogs live in **rainforests** or in lakes or rivers. Others live on **mountains** or in hot, dry deserts.

mountains   very big hills made of rock

rainforests   forests with many trees and lots of rain

Green frogs eat insects, slugs, snails, and small snakes

Most frogs eat insects. Big frogs also eat snakes, mice, birds, and fish. Frogs catch **prey** with their long, sticky tongues. Then they pull the prey into their mouths.

prey animals that are killed and eaten by other animals

Tadpoles may be eaten by fish, birds, or other animals

Most female frogs lay eggs in or near water. Tadpoles come out of the eggs. They have a tail and no legs. They breathe through **gills**. After a few weeks, the tadpoles grow legs and **lungs**. They lose their tails. Now they are adult frogs. Most wild frogs live two to three years.

gills openings in a tadpole's skin that let it get air out of water

lungs body parts used for breathing air

Frogs spend part of the day warming their bodies in the sun. If they get too hot, they might move into the shade or the water to stay cool. Many frogs are the most active at night.

Dark colors and patterns make some frogs hard to find

Frogs can be noisy! Some frogs croak, chirp, or whistle. Others buzz, hum, squeak, or honk. Males make sounds to call females or to tell other males to stay away. Some female frogs can make sounds, too.

Male frogs may have a vocal sac to make loud noises

Many people keep frogs as pets. Others like to see frogs in the wild or in zoos. These high-jumping animals are fun to watch!

Frogs have special eyelids that keep their eyes safe

A *Frog Story*

Why do frogs croak? People in Australia told a story about this. Frog thought he was the best singer ever. He believed his music was so pretty it could make the moon fall out of the sky. Every night, Frog sang to the moon. But the moon never noticed. One night, Frog sang so loud that he lost his voice—only a croak came out. He has croaked ever since.

Read More

Frisch, Aaron. *Frogs*. Mankato, Minn.: Creative Education, 2014.

Riggs, Kate. *Frog*. Mankato, Minn.: Creative Education, 2013.

Websites

Kidzone: Frogs
http://www.kidzone.ws/lw/frogs/
This site has lots of frog facts and pictures.

San Diego Zoo Kids: Blue Poison Frog
http://kids.sandiegozoo.org/animals/amphibians/blue-poison-frog
Learn more about blue poison frogs.

Note: Every effort has been made to ensure that the websites listed above are suitable for children, that they have educational value, and that they contain no inappropriate material. However, because of the nature of the Internet, it is impossible to guarantee that these sites will remain active indefinitely or that their contents will not be altered.

Index